Place baby's photo here.

This album belongs to

....

Life before you

Even before we knew you were coming to join our family, we already thought of you often. Here's how we imagined you:

....
....
....
....
....
....
....
....

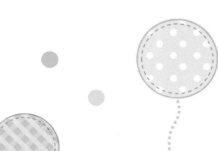

Place photo
here.

Mom

My name is ....

I was born on ....

in ....

Here is a little bit about my life
before you were born:

....

....

....

....

Place photo
here.

Dad

My name is ....

I was born on ....

in ....

Here is a little bit about my life
before you were born:

....

....

....

....

How did we meet each other?

....

....

Your family tree

Here are the members of your immediate family.

When you were born,
the whole family took you in
their arms: Here is a little
family tree to remember
everyone who already loved
you. They will have lots to
tell you when you grow up!
Your grandparents may
even tell you stories about
the silly things we did
when we were babies . . .
But don't get any ideas!

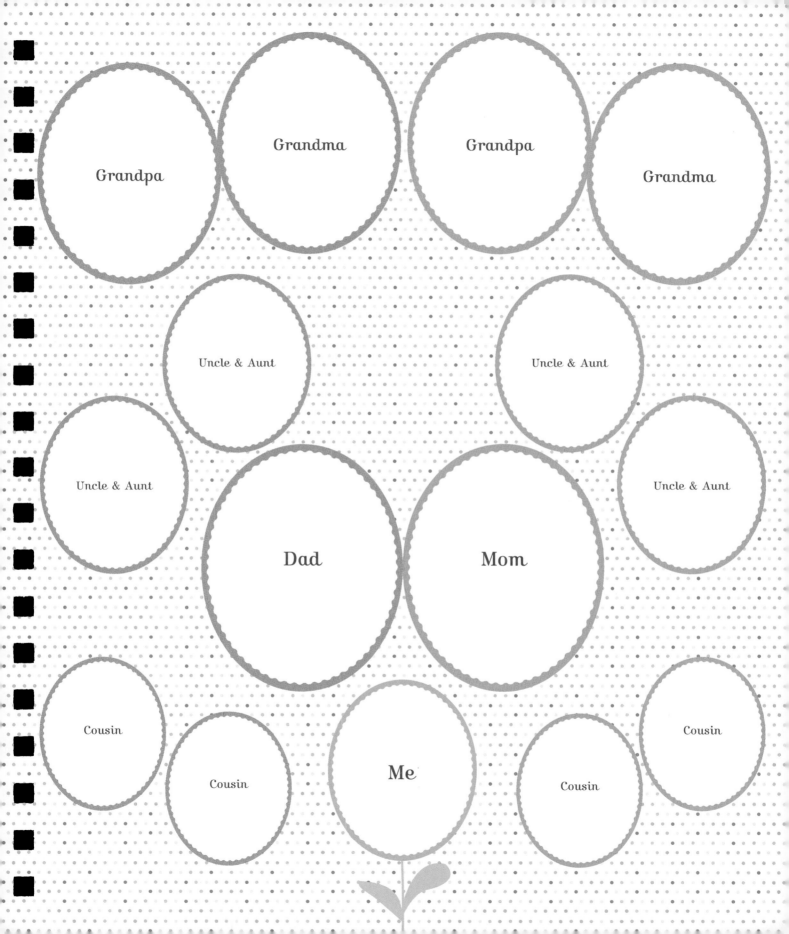

Grandpa

Grandma

Grandpa

Grandma

Uncle & Aunt

Uncle & Aunt

Uncle & Aunt

Uncle & Aunt

Dad

Mom

Cousin

Cousin

Me

Cousin

Cousin

Brothers and sisters . . .

. . . one, two, three, or a whole tribe!

They were all there to welcome you.

Their name(s) and age(s) when you were born: ....

....

....

....

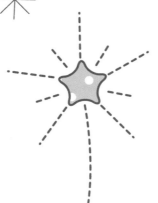

Place photos of brothers and sisters here.

They are here to watch over you

Godmother

Place photo here.

My name is: ....

I was born on: ....

in ....

Here is a little bit about my life
before you were born:

....

....

....

Godfather

Place photo here.

My name is: ....

I was born on: ....

in ....

Here is a little bit about my life
before you were born:

....

....

....

The Big News

Announcing your arrival

In an instant, our lives were changed forever.
When we learned you were coming, the most beautiful adventure
of our lives began, thanks to you!

A few words from your parents

When I found out I was pregnant on
/   /   , my reaction was:

....

....

And when I shared this great news
with your dad, his reaction was:

....

....

....

A few words from your loved ones

The reaction from ....

....

....

The reaction from ....

....

....

The reaction from ....

....

Preparing for your arrival

Little by little, we picked out Onesies,
stuffed animals, and more to welcome you . . .

Maybe your brother(s) and sister(s)
even had things to share with you?

Here's how we made a place for you in our home.

What we bought for you:

....
....
....
....
....
....
....
....

We made a lot of improvements at home!

....
....
....
....
....
....
....
....
....
....

Place a photo of preparing for baby's arrival here.

We already had so many things at home . . .

....
....
....
....
....
....
....
....
....
....
....
....
....
....

Your baby shower

It's true, all our family and friends came to the party! Before you were born, here are some of the gifts you received:

....
....
....
....
....
....
....
....
....
....
....
....
....

Place photos from the
baby shower here.

Your name

After endless discussions, here are the names
we finally agreed on:

....
....
....
....
....
....
....
....
....
....
....
....
....

Mom's favorite names
for a girl:

....
....
....
....
....
....

Mom's favorite names
for a boy:

....
....
....
....
....
....

Dad's favorite names
for a boy:

....
....
....
....
....
....

Dad's favorite names
for a girl:

....
....
....
....
....
....

Your first pictures

Two little feet, ten little fingers, one beating heart . . .
This is the story of seeing you for the first time.
Dad said you looked like him already!
And Mom was so proud to be carrying you in her belly.

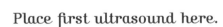

Place first ultrasound here.

Here are your other ultrasounds.

Mom's belly at 5 months.

Mom's belly at 8 months.

Your room

We created a space just for you. A crib, changing
table, dresser . . . We made it so you had a place
in our home, which was yours now, too!

Here is a picture of your room.

Finally All
Together

You are finally here!

Place the first baby
photo here.

Your name:

....

You were born on:

....

At this hospital:

....

At this time:

....

Your weight:

....

Your hair color:

....

Your length:

....

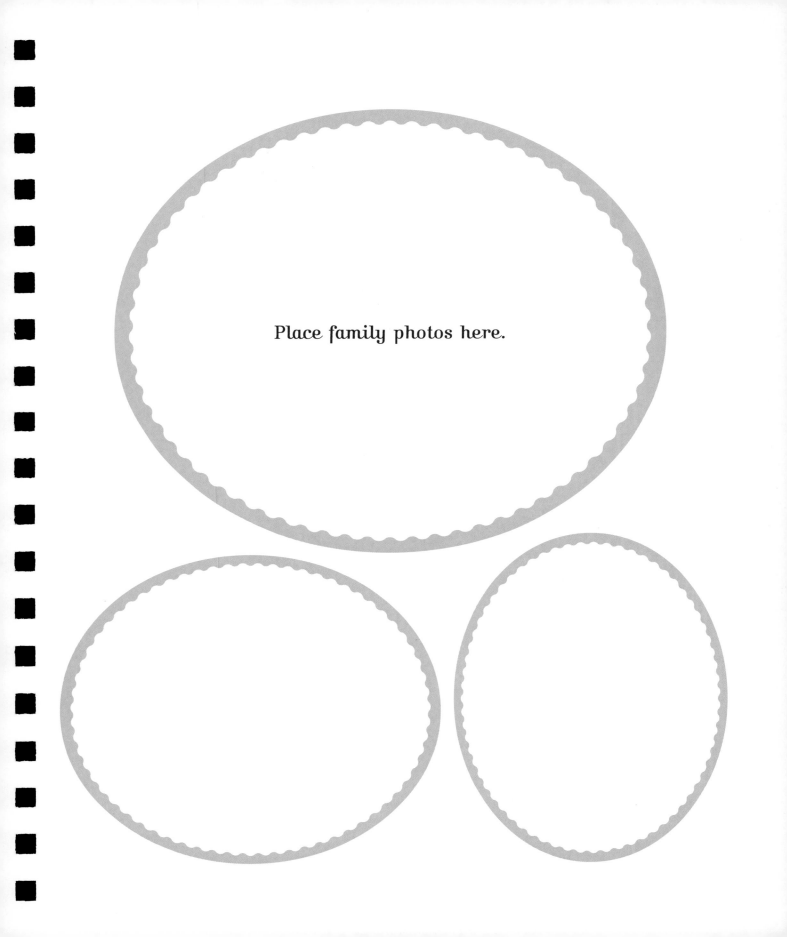

Place family photos here.

Memories from the hospital

Some photos, your hospital bracelet, an article from the newspaper, receipts from what we bought that day . . .

The moment you were born:

....
....
....
....
....
....
....
....
....
....
....

Your first moments with us:

....
....
....
....
....
....
....
....
....

Your first visitors:

....
....
....
....
....
....
....
....
....
....
....

Family resemblance

"She looks just like her grandmother!"
"He is the spitting image of his father . . ."
Everyone had their own opinion on
who you looked like.

When you were born, you looked a lot like:

....

....

But also like: ....

....

....

Your eyes reminded us of: ....

....

Your mouth looked like: ....

....

Your nose looked like: ....

....

Place photos of you and of us
when we were babies here.

You were born under a lucky star

The date and time of your birth have marked
our lives forever. But perhaps they may also
influence your personality?

Your zodiac sign is:

....

Your Chinese zodiac sign is:

....

Are you bullheaded like a Taurus? Calm like an Aquarius? Gentle like a Virgo? Certain parts of your personality seem to be tied to your astrological sign . . . Would you like to know which ones?

....
....
....
....
....
....
....
....
....
....
....
....
....
....

A year like no other

The little
memory book of
20__

Welcome
Home!

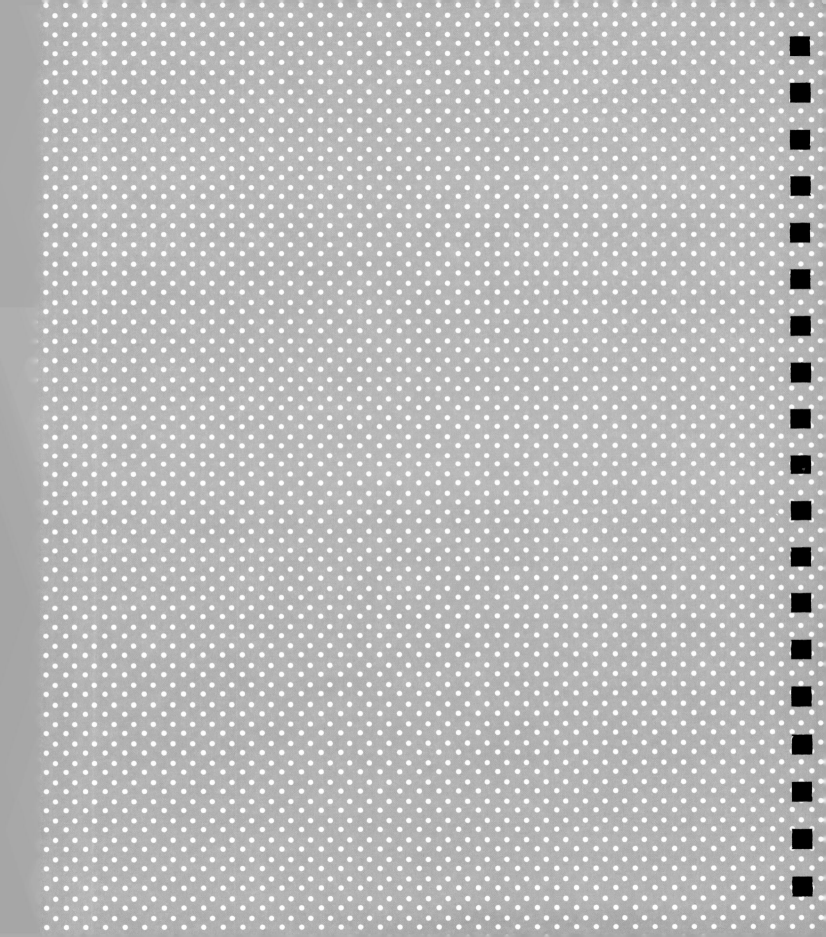

Finally home!

You came home on ....
We lived at ....

Who was patiently waiting there for you?

....
....
....

Were you bottle or breastfed?

....
....
....

If you cried, we comforted you by:

....
....
....

At home for the first time

A photo of all of us, in your new room

Your first visits!

Everyone was so excited to come over and see you.
Your first visitors were:

....

....

....

....

....

....

....

....

....

....

....

....

Here are some of the gifts we received for you:

Your birth announcement

A few photos, a keepsake card, a pretty envelope,
and voilà!

Here's how we announced the best news
in the whole world: you.

Special delivery!

Place the birth announcement here.

That was fast! Beautiful, isn't it?

Aside from this official card, we quickly started giving you plenty of nicknames of all kinds. Here are a few: ....

....

....

....

....

Good night, little one!

After many sleepless nights rocking you, feeding you,
and singing lullabies, a miracle happened . . .

You slept through the night!

Your first nights:

....
....
....
....
....
....
....
....
....
....

What helped
you fall asleep:

....
....
....
....
....
....
....
....
....
....

Your first bath

One bubble, two drops, three splashes,
it's bath time! A special bonding moment that
Mom and Dad shared with you.

Your
reactions:

....
....
....
....
....
....
....
....

Who gave you
your first bath?

....
....
....
....

Here you are
in the bath!

Place a photo of
baby's bath here.

Baby grows up

The more time passed, the more you transformed. Little by little, you grew and became heavier in our arms. Look at your progress on this fun growth chart we kept for you!

At 2 months, your height was .... and your weight was ....

At 4 months, your height was .... and your weight was ....

At 6 months, your height was .... and your weight was ....

At 8 months, your height was .... and your weight was ....

At 10 months, your height was .... and your weight was ....

At 12 months, your height was .... and your weight was ....

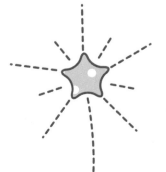

Growth Chart

. . . .

3'

A day in the life

Between visits, walks, hugs, and feedings, you didn't have a minute to spare. Here's a snapshot of 24 hours of your busy life!

1 AM	9 AM	5 PM ....
2 AM	10 AM	6 PM ....
3 AM	11 AM	7 PM ....
4 AM	Noon	8 PM ....
5 AM	1 PM	9 PM ....
6 AM	2 PM	10 PM ....
7 AM	3 PM	11 PM ....
8 AM	4 PM	Midnight ....

So Many
Firsts

First memories

You discovered the world with us, and you were in awe.
We were so happy to see you open your eyes to your surroundings!

Your first lock of hair

Your first smiles: ....
....
Your first babblings: ....
....
The first time you sat up by yourself: ....
....
....
The first time you crawled: ....
....
....
The first time you waved bye-bye: ....
....
....
The first time you made us laugh: ....
....
....
....
....

Place photos of baby's firsts here.

A spoon, a fork . . .

A spoon for Mom,
a spoon for Dad …
Mmm, it's delicious!
You're a true gourmet,
cheeks smeared with carrots!

Menu

How you behaved during your first meal: ....
....
....

Who fed you? ....
Dad with an airplane spoon, Mom with a choo-
choo train . . . Here's how we fed you: ....
....
....

The foods you liked: ....
....

The foods you hated: ....
....

What was your favorite food? ....

Your first teeth

Where did your first tooth come in? ....
....
....
....

And the next? ....
....
....
....

Whom did you bite first? ....
....
....
....

A photo of you with your first tooth

Your first vacation

Here is one of our sweetest earliest memories.
By the sea, in the mountains, or in a hotel,
here's what we did on our first family vacation.

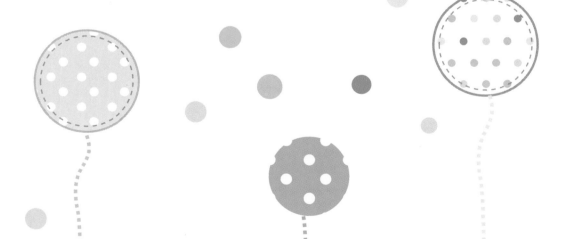

Destination: ....

The special things we brought in your suitcase:

....

Your mood during the trip: ....

....

Family activities we took part in: ....

....

....

....

Your favorite parts of the trip: ....

....

....

....

Here you are,
ready to go!

Your first holiday

The lights were twinkling, and you received so many gifts!

Where did we spend it? ....
....

Who was there? ....
....

What presents did you receive? From whom? ....
....

How did you react? ....
....

Place some photos from the
wonderful moment here!

Eventually, we had to leave you with a sitter so we could go back to work. Here's what happened:

....

....

Where did you sleep? ....

....

Who was your first babysitter? ....

....

How did you take being away from us? ....

....

How did you react the first morning without us?

....

What new things did you discover? ....

....

Your First Year

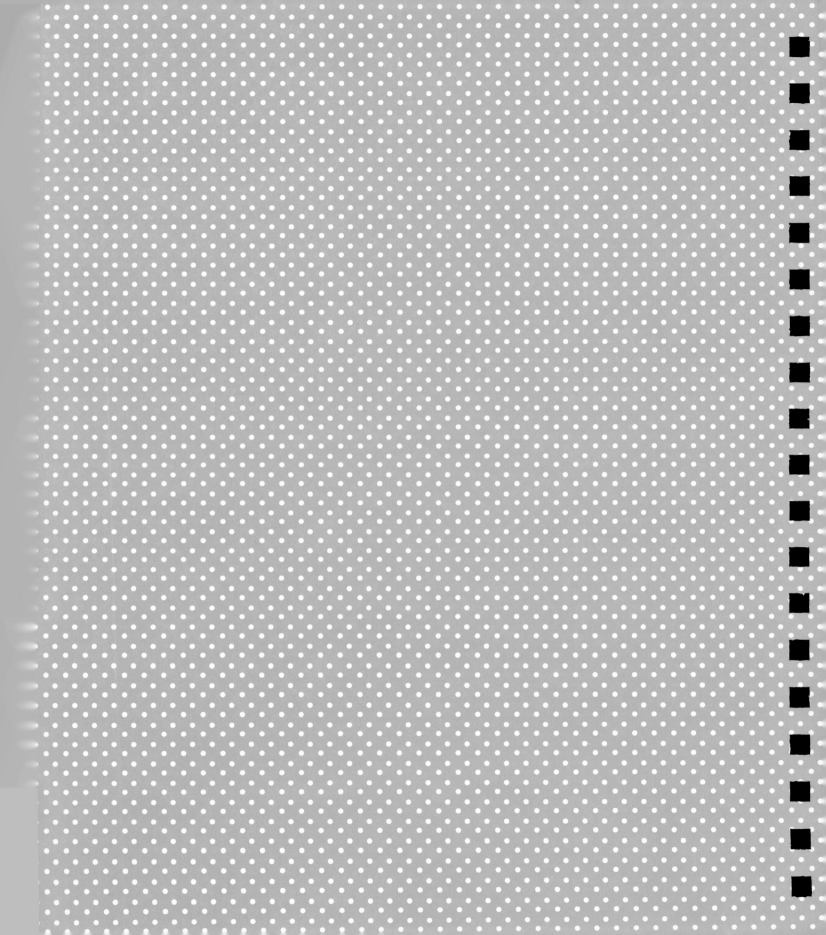

What a busy year it's been!

Here is a scrapbook of your first year, which was so important to starting your life off well. You grew so quickly, and we wanted to keep some memories of every significant moment.

Month by month, you'll discover what made us laugh or cry, how you came to learn new things, the games you liked best, and plenty of pictures of your adorable face!

Month 1

What happened your first month?

....

....

What did you do for the first time?

....

....

Who came to see you?

....

....

What was the most moving moment for us?

....

....

What were our biggest fears this month?

....

....

Month 2

What happened your second month?

....

....

What did you do for the first time?

....

....

What was a memorable moment?

....

....

Did you cry a lot?

....

....

What made us laugh the most?

....

....

Month 3

What happened your third month?

....

....

What did you do for the first time?

....

....

What made you smile the most?

....

....

How did you sleep at night?

....

....

Here are some stories that stand out from this month:

....

....

Memories from your first three months

Place photos from baby's
first three months here.

Month 4

What happened your fourth month?

....

....

What did you do for the first time?

....

....

What did you love to hold in your hands?

....

....

What new problems did we face?

....

....

What made us laugh the most?

....

....

Month 5

What happened your fifth month?

....

....

What did you do for the first time?

....

....

What fascinated you the most?

....

....

What frustrated you the most?

....

....

What was the most moving moment for us?

....

....

Month 6

What happened your sixth month?

....

....

What did you do for the first time?

....

....

What did you love putting in your mouth?

....

....

Did you sleep well?

....

....

What was the most memorable moment
from this month?

....

....

Memories from these three months

Month 7

What happened your seventh month?

....

....

What did you do for the first time?

....

....

Did you start to recognize your name?

....

Could you recognize yourself in the mirror?

....

....

Here are some gestures and sounds you made when you were hungry, when you were angry, and when you wanted to play . . . You developed quite the vocabulary!

....

....

....

....

Month 8

What happened your eighth month?

....

....

What did you do for the first time?

....

....

How did you start to move around?

....

....

What were your favorite toys?

....

....

What was the most moving moment for us?

....

....

Month 9

What happened your ninth month?
....
....

What did you do for the first time?
....
....

What did you discover about the world?
....
....

Did you cry a lot this month? Why?
....
....

What made us laugh the most?
....
....

Memories from these three months

Month 10

What happened your tenth month?

....

....

What did you do for the first time?

....

....

What was your favorite food?

....

....

Did you start to stand on your own? When?

....

....

Did you act silly this month?

....

....

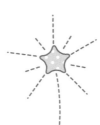

Month 11

What happened your eleventh month?

....

....

What did you do for the first time?

....

....

Did you like to imitate adults? Who inspired you most?

....

....

What food did you like the least?

....

....

What was the most memorable moment this month?

....

....

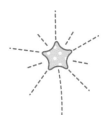

Month 12

What happened your twelfth month?

....

....

What did you do for the first time?

....

....

Did you learn to say *NO*? Did you say it often?

....

....

Did you learn to walk?

....

....

What made us laugh the most?

....

....

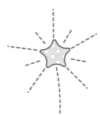

Memories from these three months

Your first birthday

It's been a whole year since you've been with us!

Where did we celebrate? ....
....

Who was there? ....
....

What gifts did you receive? From whom? ....
....

Were you able to blow out your candle? ....
....

Place photos from baby's
first birthday here!

Already a year with you!

Your handprint

Your footprint

Your favorite activities

There once was a little child who just started
to discover the big, wide world.
Games, songs, animals, nature . . .
And so much more to explore!
Here are things you liked to do.

What were
your favorite games?

....
....
....
....
....
....
....

What were
your favorite nursery
rhymes to sing?

....
....
....
....
....

Who did you
love to play with?

....
....
....
....
....
....
....

What games
did you play by
yourself?

....

....

....

....

....

....

What were your
favorite books?

....

....

Who read to you?

....

....

....

What music
did you like to
dance to?

....

....

....

....

....

....

Who were your friends?

....
....
....
....
....
....

Place a picture of baby's friends here.

Your first steps

One foot in front of the other, to catch a ball
or run into Mom's arms . . .
Look how you walked like a big kid!

Some unforgettable dates . . .

The first time you sat up:

....

The first time you stood up:

....

The first time you walked: ....

....

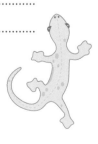

Your Second Year

Ready for your second year!

Your first birthday has come and gone, and you're
ready to start adventuring! In this scrapbook you'll
find stories from the second year of your life, all
colorful and happy. You started running, climbing,
and babbling about everything. . . How you spoiled
us being so cute! And like always, we didn't
forget to capture these moments with
plenty of photographs.

12 to 18 months

So many things happened!

What happened during this period? ....
....
....

What did you do for the first time? ....
....
....

What made you most curious? ....
....

What was your favorite meal? ....
....

What was the most moving moment for us? ....
....

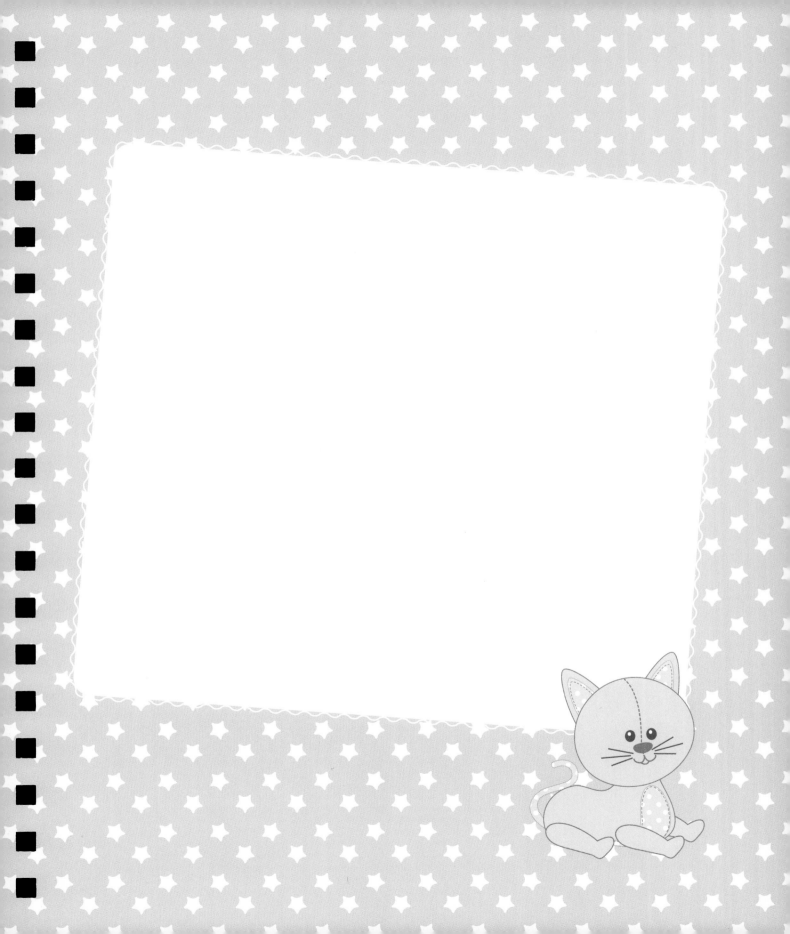

12 to 18 months

Did you make new friends? ....
....
....

Who spoiled you the most? ....
....

Did you start getting jealous? ....
....

What was your favorite toy? ....
....

What made us laugh the most? ....
....

18 to 24 months

You didn't stop growing and changing—it's been such a long time since you were just a little baby!

What happened during this period? ....
....
....

What did you do for the first time? ....
....
....

What were your biggest discoveries? ....
....
....

What words did you repeat all the time? ....
....

What was the most moving moment for us? ....
....

18 to 24 months

What was your favorite blankie or stuffed animal?

....

....

What meal did you refuse to eat all the time?

....

....

What made you laugh? ....

....

Who were your new friends? ....

....

....

Did we go on a family trip? ....

....

Place family photos here.

Your second birthday

Get out the candles, it's your birthday!
We wanted everything to be perfect
for your celebration.

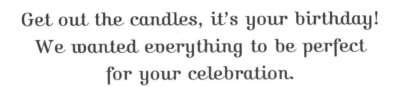

How did you spend the day? ....
....
....

Who was there? ....
....
....

What was your favorite kind of cake? ....
....

What gifts did you receive? Which did you play with
right away? ....
....

How did we feel? ....
....

Your favorite activities

Who were your friends?

....

....

....

....

....

Place a photo of baby and friends here!

What were
your favorite games?

....
....
....
....
....
....

What were
your favorite nursery
rhymes?

....
....
....
....
....

Who did
you like to play
with most?

....
....
....
....
....
....

What were your
favorite books?

....

....

Who read to you?

....

....

....

What music
did you like to
dance to?

....

....

....

....

....

....

What games
did you play by
yourself?

....

....

....

....

....

....

Place photos of baby and friends here!

Place favorite memories from
baby's first two years here.

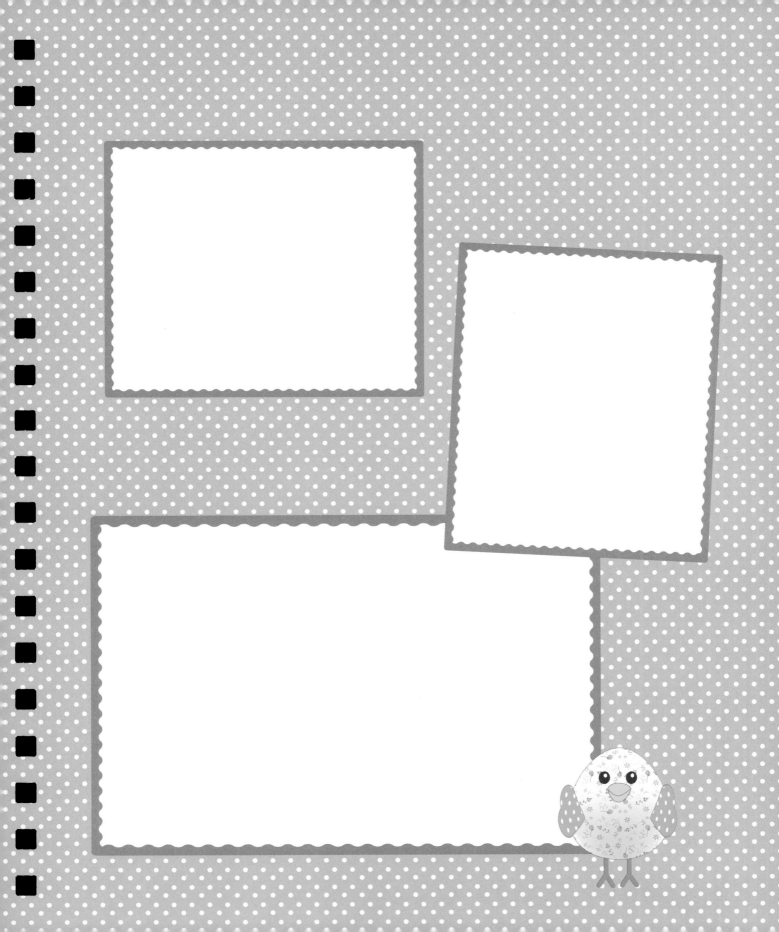

Your sparkling personality

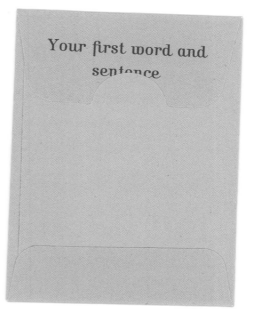

Every day we witnessed tiny miracles with you. But certain ones were truly incredible!

Photos of your best expressions

Your first word and sentence

Here are the most beautiful drawings you made
this year. What an artist you are!

And now, the end . . . .

Here's something for you to find
when you grow up!

Some sweet words
and secrets, from
us to you . . .